JOSÉ FEEDS THE WORLD

How a Famous Chef Feeds Millions of People in Need Around the World

Words by David Unger

Illustrated by Marta Álvarez Miguéns

duopress

an imprint of ⓢ sourcebooks

To José Andrés: in gratitude

—David Unger

To my grandmother, whom I still remember
every time I eat a piece of Galician bread
—Marta Álvarez Miguéns

Published by duopress, an imprint of Sourcebooks
P.O. Box 4410, Naperville, Illinois 60567-4410
(630) 961-3900
sourcebookskids.com

Cataloging-in-Publication Data is on file with the Library of Congress.

Source of Production: 1010 Printing Asia Limited, Kwun Tong, Hong Kong, China
Date of Production: September 2023
Run Number: 5034679

Printed and bound in China
OGP 10 9 8 7 6 5 4 3 2 1

José Ramón Andrés Puerta was born in Asturias, in Spain. José's parents were both nurses. He spent much of his childhood in hospitals seeing doctors and nurses helping sick people. He realized that it was possible to make life better for others in big and small ways.

When José was three, he liked helping his parents cook by peeling onions and scrubbing carrots in the *cocina*—the kitchen—after school.

His mom prepared simple but delicious meals for the family, while his dad made huge pans of *paella*—a Spanish dish with rice, chicken, sausage, shrimp, and peppers—to share with friends and family on weekends. José saw how food could make sad people feel better.

The cocina was his favorite room of the house. When he was five, José decided he wanted to be the cook. He wanted the smell of rice, saffron, chicken, and sausage to float through the air, tickling everyone's throats and getting his neighbors to sing and dance.

His dad told him that before cooking, he needed to tend the fire
for the paella pan. "My son, if you control the fire, then you can do
any cooking you want." José didn't like this answer—he wanted to
be the chef!—but in time, he realized his dad had taught him an
important lesson.

When José was fifteen, he moved to Barcelona, Spain, to enter a cooking school to become a *cocinero*—the person who cooks in the cocina. He was so creative that he got a job as a chef's assistant at El Bulli, one of the most famous restaurants in the world!

When he was twenty-one, he left Spain for New York to cook in a Spanish restaurant.

Three years later, he moved to Washington, D.C., and opened Jaleo, a restaurant that introduced *tapas*—small hot or cold snack plates—to the United States. He liked tapas because they created a community where people could share and talk and laugh!

Jaleo was the first of José's many restaurants. His dream of inventing his own recipes came true. Chef Andrés started to experiment with new ways of cooking, combining ingredients—like grapes and breadcrumbs with his fried sausages—in creative ways! Soon he started receiving awards for his culinary work.

In Washington, he also began volunteering in a soup kitchen.

Cooking for people who needed help filled his heart with joy.

Once again, he noticed how food could make people feel better.

In 2010, a terrible earthquake hit Haiti. He saw news reports of people
losing their homes and having no food and no water—many were dying,
and many more had no place to live. And no food to eat. He needed to help.

But José couldn't do the work alone.

So, he convinced a few friends to go with him.

At first, he cooked beans as he did in Spain, but the Haitians taught him to puree the beans the way they liked to eat them. He learned the lesson that it was important to cook food in the local style to make people feel better cared for and to build a community.

When he returned to Washington, D.C., he knew he needed to come up with a plan to help even more people. This is when he decided to create the nonprofit World Central Kitchen. His idea was to take everything he learned in the soup kitchen and use it to make a global organization that could provide free meals to people living in places affected by earthquakes, hurricanes, disease, and even war.

When Hurricane Maria hit Puerto Rico in 2017, José Andrés took a backpack with three days' worth of clothes and joined his World Central Kitchen team on the island. Puerto Rico was hit pretty hard. There was no electricity, and many people were homeless.

José and the team of World Central Kitchen couldn't do the work alone. And other nonprofit organizations didn't have a plan to feed the millions of people affected by the hurricane. So, he got local people to volunteer. Together they made thousands of sandwiches.

He saw opportunities where people saw problems. "I cook and I feed," he said over and over. "I boil water, then add fish and vegetables."

He wanted to help even more people.

But sometimes when there is a really big disaster,

there aren't even kitchens to cook in.

How could he do more?

After Hurricane Dorian destroyed the Abaco Islands in the Bahamas in 2019, he realized that he needed to create a food distribution system based on what was happening on the ground.

He could fly in stoves, generators, and pots to the Bahamas. But since the crops were destroyed, there wouldn't be fresh ingredients to cook with.

He needed to find another solution. The answer was to offer MREs—
Meals Ready to Eat—including food like sandwiches and apples.

When the Volcán de Fuego (Fire Volcano) erupted in Guatemala, he realized he needed to find a way to get people who were in trouble to feel their own power. "It's worth taking a risk to feed people," he said.

He thought long and hard! He knew that if he could get people to use their skills, like growing corn or beans or shopping and cooking for large families, they could become leaders in their own communities and help others as they helped themselves.

Whenever José Andrés goes to a new place where people are hungry, he gets motivated because he remembers his father wearing a white apron and cooking paella.

José can see his neighbors, young and old, eating, laughing, and even dancing.

Over the years, José Andrés has learned new lessons. In 2020, he set up a kitchen for the Navajo Nation during the worldwide COVID-19 pandemic. The Navajo live in isolated communities far from hospitals in New Mexico, Arizona, and Utah.

They were very hard hit, especially the grandmothers and grandfathers. It would be terrible if the old people, the Elders, were to disappear since they conserve the heritage and memories of the entire Navajo Nation.

He also set up kitchens in California's fields during the pandemic.

Food pickers were considered essential workers, but no one was

helping them survive.

When he arrived in New York City, where many people were sick with COVID in 2020, he set up a distribution system to feed tens of thousands of hospital workers. His memories of his parents gave him so many good ideas.

Five days after Russia invaded Ukraine in 2022, the people of Ukraine

left their homes. Everything was confusing, but World Central Kitchen was there.

José Andrés was there.

In Ukraine, World Central Kitchen keeps people fed in a country that for centuries has been feeding the world corn and wheat. By truck, by train, by car, by van: People are being fed.

José asked the Ukrainian people to become Food Fighters—4,500 volunteers, mostly women and teenagers, stepped up! It was a very difficult situation, but José Andrés felt so proud to get a country to help its own.

As long as there's hunger, José Andrés will be cooking, organizing,

and making people feel that his calling—to feed the world—is also theirs.

And one day you, too, will find your calling and
make the world a better place.

Here are some of the many recognitions that José Andrés has received as a chef and for his work with World Central Kitchen (WCK).

The **James Beard Foundation**, an organization that celebrates the best chefs in the United States, named José **Outstanding Chef** in 2011, and in 2018 presented him with the award for **Humanitarian of the Year** for his work with WCK.

Time magazine named José **One of the World's 100 Most Influential People** in 2012 and in 2018.

The **National Endowment for the Humanities** awarded José the **National Humanities Medal** in 2015.

In 2018, José was nominated for the **Nobel Peace Prize** for his humanitarian work.

In 2021, José and WCK were awarded Spain's **Princess of Asturias Award** in the Concord category.

José received the **Courage and Civility Award** from Jeff Bezos, Amazon's founder, in 2021. The award included US$100 million for WCK.

In 2022, the film *We Feed People*, about José and WCK, received two **Emmy** nominations.

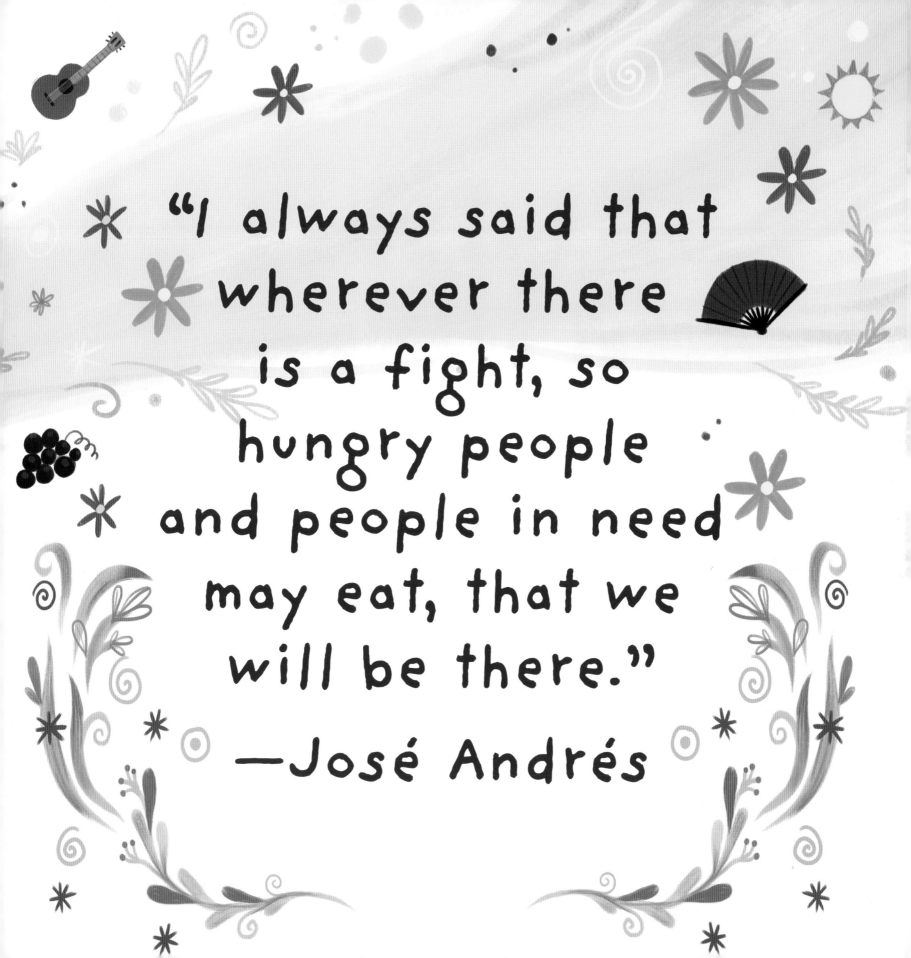

"I always said that wherever there is a fight, so hungry people and people in need may eat, that we will be there."

—José Andrés

Glossary

civility — politeness or courteous behavior

cocina — the Spanish word for "kitchen"

cocinero — the Spanish word for "chef"

community — a particular area where people live, or a group of people with common interests

COVID-19 — a serious disease that spread around the world in 2020

culinary — having to do with cooking

distribution system — procedures and activities involved with the movement of goods and services to people who need them

Elders — the older people in a group or community

generator — a machine that produces electricity

humanitarian — a person who wants to help others and cares about their welfare

humanities — areas of knowledge that deal with humans and culture

nonprofit — describes an organization or company, often devoted to humanitarian causes, that does not make a profit, or extra money

paella — a traditional Spanish rice dish, cooked in a large, round pan, to be shared on the table

pandemic — a widespread disease that travels around the world

puree — to turn a food into a thick liquid

saffron — a yellow cooking spice made from the crocus plant

tapas — small plates of food served in restaurants